THE HEART OF THE PROBLEM

ALUN EBENEZER

EP Books (Evangelical Press), Registered Office: 140 Coniscliffe Road, Darlington, Co Durham DL3 7RT

admin@epbooks.org

www.epbooks.org

EP Books are distributed in the USA by:

JPL Books, 3883 Linden Ave. S.E., Wyoming, MI 49548

order@jplbooks.com

www.jplbooks.com

British Library Cataloguing in Publication Data available

Print ISBN 978-1-78397-266-1

CONTENTS

1

THE PROBLEM

Whatever your background, political viewpoint, disposition, economic wellbeing, social standing, family circumstance, education, worldview, nationality, religion, race or culture, the one thing we can all agree on is that something is wrong with the world we live in.

It is a world full of evil, pain and sadness. Marriages and families break up, addiction takes hold of people, pornography dominates the internet, paedophilia, rape, murder, lies, deceit, theft, greed, the abuse of power, are all around us. Rates of depression, mental illness, suicide and anxiety among children and young people are on the increase. People get ill, suffer pain and heartache; natural disasters leave countries and peoples devastated.

It is a world that knows no peace. Wars and terrorist attacks are never far away. It has been estimated that in the last 4,000 years there have been less than 300 years without a major war.

Politicians let us down and despite all our best efforts to improve our lives, things don't seem to be getting any better.

We bow down to fame, power, body image, money and sex, believing they will make us happy, fulfil us and satisfy us, but they don't. We cannot seem to find ultimate satisfaction. The best the world can offer and the biggest achievements we can possibly have, all fail to fulfil our deepest needs. The actor Jim Carey said, 'I wish all people could get rich and famous and have all they ever dreamed of, so they would know it is not the answer.'

Markus Persson, the creator of *Minecraft*, described himself as a miserable billionaire, trapped in a world as lonely as the one he created. He has been on a spending spree in which he has bought everything from a fleet of supercars to a 23,000 square-foot Beverly Hills mansion that cost £46m. But it has not made him happy.

2

THE DIAGNOSIS

All of us need a doctor at some time, and when we do we tell the doctor what our symptoms are. Having done that we have one immediate requirement—a diagnosis. Nothing can go ahead without that: an accurate diagnosis points the way to understanding what is wrong and what needs to be done to put things right.

It's clear enough that the world has problems, but all these problems are just the symptoms of a deeper problem. To get a diagnosis, we need someone outside of us who can give us a reliable understanding of our deepest problem. The Bible provides that level of understanding because it God's Word, written by many people all of whom were directed and guided by God. It says that the problem is not 'out there' but rather *in us*; every one of us. The fundamental problem is not bad parents, bad schools, bad friends, bad circumstances, corrupt politicians or a broken society. The fundamental problem is we all have a bad heart.

The Bible says our heart—our inmost self—is deceitful above all things and desperately sick (Jeremiah 17:9). All of the problems we face in the world today are just symptoms of that great problem. There is a simple word used in the Bible for the cause of these symptoms; the word is *sin*.

The Fall

The very first chapter of the first book of the Bible makes it clear that originally God created the heavens and the earth and everything in them, and as he made them they were all perfect. What happened? The Bible tells us that the reason the world we live in is no longer perfect and we are in such a mess is down to something called *the fall*. Through the fall, sin entered the world. The events are recorded in the third chapter of the first book of the Bible, Genesis. God had placed the first man and woman, Adam and Eve, in a garden called Eden. It was paradise. They could eat of any fruit in the garden except from the tree of the knowledge of good and evil. If they ate from this tree they would die (Genesis 2:17). It was a clear command and warning from God. However, the Devil came to Eve in the form of a serpent and deceived her into eating the forbidden fruit and she in turn gave some to Adam. Adam and Eve therefore disobeyed God and sin and death entered the world. According to the book of Romans in the Bible (5:12), *through one man sin entered the world, and death through sin, and thus death spread to all men, because all sinned.* This was the fall.

Because Adam and Eve were the first of the whole human race, what affected them affected everyone born after them. As a result, you and I were born with sin as part of our nature. The fall is not just history: the consequences of sin and the fall are enormous and always present. Fear, evil, pain and blame entered the world because of sin. It separates us from God, who is perfect; sin makes us dirty. Relationships break down, shame is felt. Just making it through life is hard.

This may all seem like a fairy tale, but look around. Every day, in every way, we live the consequences of the fall. British theologian Jim Packer wrote '...the fall narrative gives the only convincing explanation of the perversity of human nature that the world has ever seen.'

Furthermore, not only human nature was damaged by the fall. Everything God made was contaminated by it, and so nature is beautiful on one hand but can be terribly destructive on the other hand. 'Natural disasters' of every kind (such as earthquakes and deadly weather events) are a result of the fall.

Human Nature

As well as Genesis Chapter 3 recording what the root problem is, every day our human nature confirms the fall is true. You know you are not right; like me, you are a sinner. We all like to think of and assess ourselves when we are at our best. But the real 'us' is when we are at our worst; when we do what comes most naturally to us. Imagine you had a day to yourself and were more attractive, had more money and could do whatever you wanted without getting found out. What would you do? Be honest. Think about it; think about what you are like when you are on your own; what you naturally do left to your own devices; how angry, nasty and jealous you get, how gossipy you can be, how dirty your mind is, how shameful some of the things you have done (or would have done given half the chance and could have got away with it!). Think about your internet history. Think about your language, your pride, how you look down on others. Think about how lazy you are. That's the real you! People get drunk and behave badly and the next day blame it on the drink. But the drunk, no inhibitions, defences down, mask off, was the real them.

Like you, it is in my nature to do what is wrong and shameful. I've got a cat called Cookie. No bird, squirrel, mouse, is safe in our garden when Cookie is out there. He's killed hundreds. I on the other hand, have not killed one. I can proudly say I have never chased one bird, squirrel or mouse around my garden and sunk my teeth into it! Killing birds and squirrels and chasing mice are not in my nature, but it is in his. However, being lustful, selfish, getting angry, gossiping, telling lies, always wanting more, all these are in my nature. I am drawn to these things and find them all too easy to indulge in.

I have been a school teacher and worked with young people for the last 21 years and this has been confirmed to me every day throughout every one of those years. I have never had to teach children to be naughty; never had to say to them, 'now this is how you tell lies, this is how not to share, this is how to punch someone in the face!' Never! They just know how to do it. These things are in the nature of every child.

Selfish

Our nature really shows itself in how selfish we are. I live in London and see this as I travel on the Underground. Everyone rushes for the Tube, desperate to either get to work on time or to get home. As hundreds of people rush to catch the Tube, all we care about is whether we get on. If I jump on the train as the doors are closing and just make it, I take a huge sigh of relief. The fact dozens didn't make it doesn't matter. I'm alright.

We are obsessed with *self*. We don't own 'youphones' or 'youpads' but 'iPhones' and 'iPads.' We don't take 'youies' but 'selfies.' I was born voting for me and you were born voting for you; I'm all about me and you are all about you.

Powerful

People often like to think of 'sin' or 'sins' as something that occasionally happens in their life but is normally under control. The real problem is that sin is not something we do or don't do; instead, sin is a power that destroys us. We like to think we do what we want but the reality is we are controlled by our sinful nature (Hebrews 2:15; Colossians 1:13).

A man sits in his room alone with his computer and just thinks he'll click on an image once. Before he knows it he is addicted to pornography. You tell some lies and before long you are a liar. The first time the alcoholic got drunk he had no plans on becoming addicted. Sin destroys lives and causes much suffering. It troubles your conscience and wracks you with guilt. It leaves you feeling dirty. Like an addict you won't think straight and will just do whatever it takes to get your fix of your particular sin. If you don't kill sin, sin will kill you. We're tangled up in our sin. We'd love to be different but we just can't seem to make ourselves better.

As you read this book, there may be a particular sin, or what you may call a habit, you really struggle with or a way of life or a relationship that you just can't give up. Maybe, probably, it is a sexual sin. When sex is involved most people—men in particular—stop thinking straight. Lust, pornography, adultery, flings, are all things people think they can control but end up being controlled by them. Every time you indulge in it you think it will be the last time, but you keep having to go back for more. But it is not just sex we are slaves to and that proves too powerful for us. It can be any number of things—hatred, jealousy and anger, selfish ambition, drunkenness, gossip, possessions. According to Henry David Thoreau, 'The things we own can own us too.'

Maybe you disagree with all this and think you are okay. Well, stop sinning today. Try it—see how you get on. I guarantee you will find you are not in control. We hate to admit it, but the reality is we are enslaved by these things.

Deceitful

The great power of sin lies in the fact that at first it appears to be so attractive and enticing. It always promises it will make us feel so good and we just have to have it. This is illustrated for us in the Bible, in the Old Testament, in the life of King David. He was at home in his palace when all his men had gone to war (2 Samuel 11). From the roof of his palace he saw a beautiful woman bathing and thought to himself, 'I have got to have her.' Her husband was away at war and when the woman, called Bathsheba, came to David at his request they began an affair. Bathsheba became pregnant, so what she and David had done was in danger of being found out. To cover up the mess, David arranged for her husband Uriah to come home from battle, thinking that he would surely spend the night with Bathsheba and so it would appear that the child was his. But Uriah was a good soldier—he would not go home and sleep with his wife while his fellow-soldiers were on the battlefield. David tried every trick, even getting Uriah drunk, but nothing worked. Desperate to cover his tracks, David arranged for Uriah to go back to war and to fight on the front line of the battle where he was killed. What started as an afternoon of fun ended up with lies, betrayal and murder. Sin isn't what it appears. It is destructive. It gives momentary pleasure but destroys people's lives.

There are so many examples of the deceitfulness and destructiveness of sin. Pubs and clubs are full of fun and excitement at the start of Friday and Saturday night but so often the result is that people have fallen out, had fights, got jealous, ended up doing things that at the time seemed so much pleasure and fun but leave them feeling guilty and burdened with wrecked marriages, families and relationships. People wake up in the middle of the night or in the morning feeling empty, hating themselves and those they've committed shameful acts with. People get infatuated with the pleasures of sin but in the end they hate themselves.

That is the great truth about sin: it promises so much but always leaves you feeling dirty and guilty. It feels so good at the time but it ruins lives, breaks up families and causes untold pain. The journalist Malcolm Muggeridge once met a woman who, he was told, had slept with the writer H G Wells. He asked her how it had happened. She told him that Wells had approached her at a party and said, "Shall we go upstairs and do something funny?" "And was it funny?" asked Muggeridge. "No sir, it was not funny," she replied. "That evening has caused me more misery than any other evening in my life."

After sinning the first feeling is often disappointment and sometimes remorse. Even the best things in life will not fulfil you totally. You could gain the whole world only to find out the world is not enough. Johnny Wilkinson (*The Times*, November 21st 2009) powerfully proves this point when he described what it was like winning the rugby world cup for England. It was the pinnacle of his career and something almost every school boy in the country dreams of. But this is what he said:

> *I had already begun to feel the elation slipping away from me during the lap of honour around the field. I couldn't believe that all the effort was losing its worth so soon. This was something I had fantasised about achieving since I was a child. In my head I had reached the peak of the mountain and now all that was left was to slowly descend the other side. I'd just achieved my greatest ambition and it felt a bit empty.*

Rebel

But the worst thing about sin is that it is rebellion against God. Someone has defined sin as '**S**hove off God, **I**'m in charge, **N**ot you.' We are rebels and hate the thought of God telling us what to do. Sin messes up my life and the lives of others but the worse thing of all is we don't love God. We act like he doesn't exist. The heart and horror of sin is that it is against God.

You may be reading this and are really thinking by now, 'So what? Why does it matter if I don't love God and act like he doesn't exist?' Well, imagine I threw a party and invited you. You came to my house and knocked at the door. I opened it but you ignored me and just pushed past me. You ate all my food, listened to my music, watched my TV, played on my snooker table and table-tennis table; played darts and table football, talked to everyone at the party, helped yourself to whatever you wanted but didn't talk to me all night. You broke some of my stuff, made a real mess of my house then left without even a 'thank you.' You'd think that was outrageous. And yet we live in God's world. He made you, every good thing you have is from him (Jame 1:17), he gives you the breath you are drawing right now and yet you act like he doesn't exist.

Guilt

But what really confirms sin is real and this diagnosis is right is the overwhelming sense of shame and guilt. Maybe sin has really destroyed your life and caused you and those you love so much suffering. Maybe your conscience is troubled and you are constantly wracked with guilt. You agree with the book of Ezra in the Bible where it says, *I am too ashamed and humiliated to lift up my face to You, my God; for our iniquities have risen higher than our heads* (Ezra 9:6) or with King David in Psalm 51 when he says, *My sin is always before me.* The lyrics of the Avett Brothers song are words under which you live, 'Shame. Boatloads of shame. Day after day. More of the same. Blame. Please lift it off. Please take it off. Please make it stop.' To live in this world is to experience shame. Boatloads of shame.

Seen

Shame comes from your conscience, but your conscience is not your biggest problem. God has seen it all. Perhaps you have managed to go undetected by those around you but God has been watching. God sees our sins. He knows them all specifically and remembers them all. One character in the Bible speaks of God as *You are the God who sees* (Genesis 16:13). I once caught a Year 7 boy called Kieron smoking behind the Technology block at school. When I asked him he denied it completely.

I remember him looking at me in total consternation that I should even think or suggest that he would do such a thing. I remember him saying to me, "Mr Ebenezer, I am so hurt you think I could do such a thing!" So I marched him by the scruff of the neck to watch the CCTV recording which showed him puffing away to his heart's content! He looked at it and said, "You're right sir, it does look a bit like me!" One day God will take each of us to his CCTV, where we will find our whole life has been recorded. But God sees more than CCTV ever could—he has seen everything you have done, heard everything you've said and even knows your every thought and intention.

Verdict

The heart of the problem is the problem of the heart. The symptoms are all around us and the diagnosis is that we are sinners, every one of us (Romans 3:23). And there is nothing we can do to stop sinning or to remove the sins we have already committed.

3

THE PROGNOSIS

You remember we began the last section by imagining a visit to the doctor where the first thing we need is a diagnosis—what is wrong? The word *prognosis* above is not so well known, but it simply means the outlook. In other words, where does the condition I have lead? What will happen if it carries on?

The Bible tells us the answer to these questions. It has already shown us what happened at the fall, and how sin now is at the root of all the troubles of the world and is affecting every one of us. So the Bible goes on to show us the prognosis, which tells us just how serious things are and why the diagnosis cannot be ignored.

Death

The Bible says, *The wages of sin is death* (Romans 3:23). Because of sin, we all have to die. In his poem, 'Death Lib', Steve Turner says,

The liberating thing about
      death
Is in its fairness to women
its acceptance of blacks,
its special consideration
for the sick.
And I like the way
that children aren't excluded,
homosexuals are welcomed,
and militants aren't banned.
Con men can't con it
Thieves can't nick it
Bullies can't scare it
Magicians can't trick it.
Boxers can't punch it
Nor critics dismiss it
Don't knows can't not know
The lazy can't miss it.
Governments can't ban it
Or the army defuse it
Judges can't jail it
Lawyers can't sue it.
Capitalists can't bribe it
Socialists can't share it
Terrorists can't jump it
The Third World aren't
      spared it.
Scientists can't quell it
Nor can they disprove it
Doctors can't cure it
Surgeons can't move it.

Einstein can't halve it
Guevera can't free it
The thing about dead
Is we're all gonna be it.

The Judgement

The diagnosis is that we are sinners. The prognosis is death, but then the Bible says that is not the end—after death, we are judged by God (Hebrews 9:27). You can try to convince yourself that after death there is nothing, but you know that is not true. If that is the case, why do we fear death? An animal just finds a corner, curls up and dies. But we know death is not the end. We try not to think about it, trivialise it or come up with our own ideas about what happens but death is terrifying. At funerals we tell ourselves, 'another one has gone next door' or 'he's on the golf course in the sky.' The most frequently requested song at funerals in 2014, according to Co-operative Funeralcare, was Monty Python's *Always look on the bright side of life*. It includes these words:

Life is quite absurd and
    death's the final word
You must always face the
    curtain with a bow
Forget about your sin—give
    the audience a grin

Enjoy it, it's your last chance
anyway.

The problem is that the song is total nonsense.
The Bible makes that quite clear by speaking often
of a day that God has set, a judgement day. You can
read a brief description in Matthew 24:30-31. That
will be a day when everyone will stand before God
and give an account of their lives. The day will
begin with a trumpet blast that everyone will hear.
The Lord Jesus Christ will return to earth and
everybody will see him, this time as a glorious King,
very different to his first coming to earth as a baby
in Bethlehem. Everyone will be summoned to this
judgement; everyone from all over the globe and
throughout history. Whether you like it or not, or
believe it or not, one day you and I will stand before
the judgement seat of God. Every great historical
figure will stand before this seat. Every king, queen
and world leader that has ever lived will stand
before this seat. Film stars, pop stars, sports men
and women will stand before this seat. Tramps,
beggars, 'ordinary' people, Asians, Americans,
Europeans, Africans, 'good people', terrorists,
rapists, murderers, will all stand before this
judgement seat.

And it won't be the judgement seat of public
opinion, or the judgement seat of modern thinking,
or the judgement seat of social media. This will be
the judgement seat of God!

Standing at the judgement seat of God will be

an awful day when the hearts of many will fail them for fear (Luke 21:26). It will be a day when everything we have done will come to light. Such will be the shame and terror that people will want the rocks and mountains to cover and fall on them and there will be a great separation (Matthew 24:40, 41).

Hell

People who stand before God on judgement day still in their sin will be condemned to an eternal hell. In the twenty-first century, even Bible-believing Christians have tried to sanitise hell and cover it up as some kind of embarrassing family secret, but hell is as real and terrifying today as it has always been. As you sit reading this book wherever you may be, there are people who once walked this earth and lived and breathed like you, but now find themselves in torment in hell.

Many people find it hard to take hell seriously, but it is a real place. A place deep down we all believe in. We all think it is right when criminals get sent to prison. No one should 'get away with it.' How much more should God punish those who have sinned against him?

Hell is the final place of those consigned to eternal punishment. It is a place of torment. A place of fire and outer darkness, where people are weeping and are in so much pain they gnash their teeth (Matthew 8:12; 13:42; 22:13; 25:30, 41; Mark

9:44). It is a place of distress and misery where people's consciences plague them throughout eternity. All the things we enjoy on earth will be gone forever. It is impossible to imagine how awful it will be; never being able to hear music ever again; never tasting good food ever again; never having your thirst quenched; absolute darkness; horrible loneliness; never feeling loved or cared for. The anger of God hanging over you forever. There is no escape, no emergency exit, no prospect of getting out. Dante said that over the gates of hell would be the words, 'Abandon hope, all ye who enter here'. What a terrible place to find yourself for all eternity!

In *The Times* (July 29th 2008) there was a report on a 20 year-old British woman, Samantha Orabator held in Phanathong prison in Laos. Inmates described conditions in the prison as squalid. Kay Danes, an Australian who spent ten months at the prison has described the abuse and neglect at the jail. "I've heard all the prisoners yelling at the top of their lungs, shouting for guards when one of the inmates was dying, and nobody comes. Nobody ever comes."

The Bible describes a place far worse than Phanathong prison where people scream at the top of their lungs but nobody comes. Nobody ever comes!

4

THE CURE

Just for a moment we go back to our visit to the doctor. We have had the diagnosis and it could not be more serious. The prognosis, the outcome if we just carried on as we are, is terrifying. We need a cure, something that will put everything that is wrong right again. The prospects do not look good: we have seen that we are up against God and that we are rebels against him. We all know we cannot avoid death, and that our death is followed by meeting God at the judgement seat, where the verdict seems to be a foregone conclusion. Where can we find any hope of a cure?

Strangely, the same Bible that warns us of death and judgement and hell holds out the cure. Just a little reading of the Bible shows that God doesn't tell us about hell because he is nasty and horrible and wants to frighten us and spoil our enjoyment; rather, out of love and kindness, he warn us about it so that we don't end up there. He wants us to understand what is wrong with us, the diagnosis;

know the danger we are in, the prognosis; and then come to him for the cure.

God so loved

As we have seen, to God sin is serious and has eternally serious consequences. He is holy and perfect and just, and his justice demands that sin is punished. But this holy God is also love, and the Bible says that God *so loved the world* (John 3:16). Incredibly, this means that God loves rebellious, dirty, messed up sinners. We do not have time to study everything in detail here, but the Bible assures that before the fall, before the world was even made, God saw what would happen and determined to save people. When the fall happened, God made the first announcement of his plan (Genesis 3:15) and as time went by, the Bible shows that he revealed more and more details of what he would do. Because of his love, God promised he would provide a cure; he would send a Saviour to rescue men and women, boys and girls from their sins. That Saviour was his own Son, the Lord Jesus Christ.

When my son was small, I used to ask him, 'How much do you love me?' At the time we lived in Cardiff and my parents lived in Ebbw Vale, about 30 miles away, and he would say to me: 'Dad, I love you all the way to Ebbw Vale!' But then he started watching 'The Koala Brothers', a children's TV show set in the Australian Outback, and he would

say to me, 'Dad, I love you all the way to Australia!'
He then progressed to watching 'Lunar Jim' and
would say, 'Dad, I love you all the way to the moon!'

Suppose you were to ask God 'How much do
you love me?' He would take you to a feeding
trough in which a baby is lying. But this is no
ordinary baby. He is fully human, born of a woman,
but at the same time fully God. In the words of the
carol, this is 'our God contracted to a span,
incomprehensibly made man.' He left heaven,
where he had been adored by the angels, where he
had been worshipped from eternity. He was given
the name 'Jesus' and he subsequently grew up in
Nazareth, a small northern village in Israel. God
says, 'That's how much I love you.'

But that's not all. He then takes you to a garden
called Gethsemane, and you see a man in turmoil.
He is facing a cruel death on a cross and is
swallowed up in sorrow, overwhelmed to the point
of collapsing and dying (Matthew 26:38). He feels
trapped and hemmed in on every side with the
horrible feeling of not being able to get out. His
soul is in such agony that he doesn't know what to
do with himself. He doesn't know how he is going
to get through what he is about to go through. He is
agitated. As he prays, he falls on his face (Matthew
26:39). The Son of God is literally 'throwing himself
to the ground' (Mark14:35). He is dreading what he
is about to face so much so that his sweat turns to
blood. Luke, who was a doctor, actually notes that
there were great drops of blood falling to the

ground (Luke 22:44). Not only was he sweating and bleeding, the creator of the universe was crying out with strong tears (Hebrews 5:7). He is arrested by a mob of 300 men with torches and lanterns and put on trial. And God says, 'That's how much I love you.'

But there's more still, because God says 'I love you all the way to Golgotha.' It means 'the place of the skull' and there you see a cross on a hill outside Jerusalem. The figure on the cross is so battered that it doesn't even look like a human being. There is a crown of thorns on his head, he is naked and has been whipped and beaten and spat at, then nails have been driven into his and his feet. It grows dark and he cries out in the darkness, *My God, my God, why have you forsaken me?* And God says to you, 'This is how much I love you.' Bethlehem, Gethsemane, Golgotha.

An Indian philosopher in explaining the difference between Islam and Christianity said that Allah was too majestic to lie in a dirty manger, hang on a shameful cross and enter filthy hearts. His adherents have to get to him. But the Bible says, look in that manger, go to that garden, survey that cross and behold your God!

In 1964 Kitty Genovese was murdered in Kew Gardens in New York. It was witnessed by thirty-eight people who saw the killer come into the park and carry out the attack. They shouted from the windows for him to stop and even though he did leave the park, he came back and killed her. When the police asked the witnesses why they didn't come down to help the lady when they saw the danger she was in, they said that they didn't want to get involved. But Jesus Christ, when he saw the mess we had made of our lives and the danger we were in didn't just shout down from Heaven, he came down, right down. He rolled his sleeves up, put on human flesh, became one of us and took on himself all our sin.

The promise of the cure

In the Old Testament—the part of the Bible before the birth of the Lord Jesus Christ—the Saviour is anticipated. This part of the Bible tells the story of the creation of the world, the flood and then the call of Abraham, (Genesis 12:1-3). The descendants of Abraham became the people of Israel, the people God chose to work through. God had promised Abraham that he would make form his descendants a great nation, and that through these people all the world would be blessed. This great promise was fulfilled when the Saviour was born (Matthew 1:1-17). Jesus Christ came from the Jews but was not just for the Jews; he would be the Saviour of the whole world—Britain, America, Japan, China, Syria, Iraq, Iran, India, Russia; people from the four corners of the earth! It doesn't matter if you are a Jew or a Gentile (non-Jew), *God so loved the world* (John 3:16). This Saviour is for everyone and is the only one recognised by

God; there is no salvation in anyone else (Acts 4:12).

The Saviour was born to a peasant, a virgin called Mary who was engaged at the time to a carpenter called Joseph. Joseph was not the father of Mary's son; the Bible tells us that she became pregnant through the wonderful work of the Holy Spirit. Joseph and Mary were told to call the boy 'Jesus' which was a fairly common name at the time. Like the Old Testament name Joshua it means 'God is salvation.' The first 30 years of his life were lived in obscurity apart from a few notable events—the visit of shepherds at his birth (Luke 2:8-20), his circumcision and dedication in the Temple (Luke 2:21-38), the visit of some wise men from the east a little later (Matthew 2) and a visit to Jerusalem with his parents when he was twelve years old (Luke 2:41-52).

When he was about 30 he began his public ministry. His arrival on the scene was announced by his forerunner, John the Baptist (Luke 3:1-20), who also baptised Jesus. As he came up from the water a voice was heard from Heaven saying, *You are My beloved Son; in You I am well pleased* (Luke 3:21, 22); this was the voice of God the Father, confirming that as well as being a fully human man, he was also fully God. Jesus Christ was and is 100% man and 100% God.

His message was *repent*—meaning 'turn away from your sin and turn to God' (Matthew 4:7). Perhaps his most famous sermon is the Sermon on the Mount where he describes what a true Christian is like (Matthew 5-7).

Jesus Christ did not come to establish a physical, geographical kingdom but a spiritual kingdom. His kingdom and rule are established in the hearts and lives of all those who believe in him. After this life believers go to be with him forever in Heaven.

Many people followed the Lord Jesus Christ for a while but then turned away (John 6.66). The religious leaders of the day opposed his teaching; they felt threatened by him and were jealous of his popularity and hated how he exposed their hypocrisy. On one level, it was these leaders, together with the Roman authorities who put him to death.

But really, behind the scenes, it was all part of God's eternal plan to save sinners (Acts 2:23). The Son of God being born of Mary, living a perfect life, dying on the cross and rising again is God's way of saving men and women, boys and girls. It is the only cure, for the heart of the problem which is the problem of our hearts. This cure is free to everyone, but it is not cheap. It cost God everything!

How the cure was provided

The four gospels are four biographies of the Lord Jesus Christ, but they differ from one important way from modern biography. All four give a large section of their account to the last few days of the life of the Lord, concentrating especially on his last few hours. Here is a summary:

Arrest and Trial

On a Thursday night after supper with his twelve disciples (often called The Last Supper), Jesus was betrayed by one of his disciples, Judas Iscariot, and arrested in a garden called Gethsemane by a large mob of about 300 people with swords and clubs, lanterns and torches. All his friends abandoned him and the Lord Jesus Christ had to go through a series of mock trials which began on that Thursday night and carried on to Friday.

First the religious leaders, then Pontius Pilate (the Roman Governor of Judea at the time), then King Herod, then Pontius Pilate again, questioned the Lord. What is clear is that they could not find any fault with Jesus. The religious leaders wanted to get rid of him; Pilate was afraid of upsetting the religious leaders and Herod was simply curious.

The Lord remained silent throughout these events. As Pilate reminded him of all the accusations, he did not speak. Pilate was used to people in this position cowering and begging, but Jesus made no reply, not even to a single charge (Matthew 27:12-14; Isaiah 53:7; Luke 23:9; John 19:9). Peter, who was present, says they hurled their insults at him but he did not retaliate; when he suffered he made no threats (1 Peter 2:22-24).

Why didn't the Lord answer and defend himself? In Roman law, silence was an admission of guilt. Jesus Christ, the eternal Son of God, by remaining silent was saying, 'I am guilty.' He had done nothing wrong himself, indeed the Bible assures us he was sinless (Hebrews 4:15), but he was pleading guilty for all your sins and mine. Jesus Christ stood trial for the sins of every man and woman, boy and girl, who trusts in him.

Sentence and punishment

It is quite clear that Pilate would have let the Lord Jesus go after a beating, but the religious leaders insisted on death by crucifixion, a Roman punishment that needed sentencing by Pilate. Pilate gave in to their demands, and so Jesus was handed over to the custody of Roman soldiers who flogged him, a brutal process that would tear the flash and even leave bone exposed. This cruel act was followed by mockery by the Roman soldiers. They dressed him as if he were a king, and in pretending to salute him they beat him and spat on him.

He who spoke and a universe came into being; he who put the planets in their place; he who built every mountain and rolled out every sea; he of whom the disciples said, *even the wind and the sea obey him* (Mark 4:41); he who was from the beginning God, subjected himself to this!

As well as all this, the soldiers weaved a crown

of thorns and placed it on his head. This would have been extremely painful and a great indignity, but this act carried great significance. In Genesis 3:18 God says that thorns and thistles would grow as a result of sin entering the world. Unbeknown to them, the soldiers were taking the symbol of human sin and weaving it into a crown for the Saviour, the one who will represent sinners under the curse of God.

Walk of shame

After being sentenced and flogged and prepared for crucifixion, Jesus then had to walk to the site of crucifixion, a place called Gologotha (in Hebrew) or Calvary (in Greek), in the north of Jerusalem, just outside the city wall. Part of the punishment imposed on the vilest criminals was that they should carry their own cross when they went to execution. In the fullest sense, the Lord Jesus was reckoned as a sinner. The pain he suffered was not just physical but psychological. He had to endure the shame of being viewed as a vile criminal. When we think of him walking through those streets whipped to the bone, bloodied with a crown of thorns on his head, carrying his cross and doing the walk of shame, we must see that he was suffering the shame and guilt that our sin deserves. He was enduring our shame!

Guilt and shame paralyse us. Psychologists say

that the biggest problem they deal with is guilt. So
many of us live our lives worried we may get found
out. Everyone of us has guilty secrets. You may be
quietly hoping and thinking you've got away with it,
but you have not. God sees and knows everything.
If you are trusting in Jesus Christ then he bore the
shame for you, but if you are not your sins will be
revealed at judgement. You must then carry the
shame and the punishment.

In the *Game of Thrones* series five finale, the
queen Ceresi was forced to walk naked through the
streets of Kings Landing as the screaming, hostile
crowd threw food and the contents of their
chamber pots at her. Lena Headey who played the
queen, had a body double to do that scene. As Jesus
was walking through the streets of Jerusalem
enduring all the shame, he was the 'body double' of
all those who trust him.

Crucifixion

Crucifixion is perhaps the worst and cruellest form
of punishment ever devised. The Roman writer
Cicero certainly thought so. He said, 'Let it never
come near the body of a Roman citizen, not even
his thoughts, his eyes or his ears.' The Romans
devised crucifixion but their law allowed it to only
be used for non-Romans. It was considered the
most shameful and disgraceful way to die.

The soldiers would have laid Jesus on the cross

and nailed him to it. They would have then lifted the cross up and dropped it into a prepared socket. Every bone in his body would have jolted and his nerves would have shivered with the excruciating pain.

The Lord's condition on the cross is described by the prophet Isaiah: people were astonished at him, probably because he was so disfigured that he was beyond human likeness (Isaiah 52:14). People hid their faces from him (Isaiah 53:3). He was horribly wounded and bruised (Isaiah 53:5). But the accounts of the crucifixion show marvellous restraint by the Gospel writers. All four of them simply say *and they crucified him*.

My God, My God

On the cross the Lord Jesus Christ was taking upon himself the wrath of a sin-hating, holy God. When they hammered him onto that cross, he was taking the hammering our sins deserve. On the cross he was saying to God in effect, 'don't punish them for their sin, don't be angry with them, take it all out on me!' As the Son of God was being sacrificed in the place of millions of sinners, under so much stress, his cry was, *'My God, my God, why have you forsaken me?'* (Matthew 27.46). There is no sadder word than 'forsaken.' Think of a widow coming home from the funeral of her husband, or a child whose parents have been killed in a car accident. If a child is in trouble, need or pain, they call out 'Dad, Dad.' But imagine dad doesn't come. Forsaken, abandoned, alone! But not even these compare with being forsaken by God in your hour of need. Jesus knew what it was like to be forsaken by men, even his disciples, but now it is God who has apparently abandoned him (see John 16.32). He was totally alone. He faced the weight of the guilt of millions of sins alone. He suffered the guilt of his people, under so much wrath, in agony, with no one for support or comfort. He felt no love or care, only wrath and anger.

The wrath that God should pour out on us, was poured out on him. When he cried out *My God My God why have you forsaken me?* God's answer in effect was, "because as long as earth lasts there will be people who will need a Saviour. You are abandoned so they don't have to be."

Going through Hell

On the cross he went through Hell. You may ask how in six hours did Jesus suffer an eternal Hell? How could the millions of sins of millions of people, each one deserving eternal Hell, be paid for in a few hours on a cross, however painful those hours may have been?

I don't know, but maybe it was something like Narnia. In the Lion the Witch and the Wardrobe, the children go through the wardrobe and enter

Narnia. They feel like they are there for thousands of years but when they come back through the wardrobe into England again they have only been away a few seconds. In Narnia, time is not the same. I think this is what happened on Calvary. On earth it was hours but as Christ went into the darkness he left time and entered eternity and suffered an eternal Hell.

What this cure provides

Propitiation

The fact that Jesus Christ went through Hell shows how angry God is with sin. It isn't the sort of anger where someone flies off the handle, but a just, steady, constant burning anger. On the cross Jesus was turning away this anger. He was extinguishing the wrath of God. The Bible uses the word *propitiation* for this (1 John 2:2). On the cross Christ pacified the wrath of God. He bore the wrath of God so that God becomes 'propitious' or favourably disposed towards us.

It isn't just that he stops God being angry towards us, but that we can know God's favour. The Old Testament sacrifices that were offered could not take away or atone for a single sin. They were pictures and pointers to what Christ would do on

Calvary. In the Old Testament the sins of a multitude of people were forgiven on the grounds of what Christ would one day accomplish on Calvary (Romans 3:25). God's wrath arose from the very first sin and continued until it was poured out on Jesus Christ. But it went further. Not only was the wrath of God against all the past sins of his people dealt with at the cross, but the wrath of God against every sin of his people from the cross until the end of time. Jesus was putting out the wrath of God against millions and millions and millions of sinners.

It is important to note that forgiving our sins isn't just a legal dilemma for God. It isn't only a case that his justice needs to be satisfied; that is, the law says that sin must be punished and therefore someone has to pay that punishment. But sin is also against the very character and being of God. He is offended by it and is angry with us, and if we are to be reconciled with God and at peace with him, this anger needs to be turned away, quenched. If we trust in Christ, not only has God stopped being angry towards us but he is now happy and pleased with us.

During these hours of darkness Christ was in torment. He had to endure the pain of bearing the sin of many (Isaiah 53:12; Hebrews 9:28). He bore our sins in his body on the tree (1 Peter 2:24), and in fact he was made sin for us (2 Corinthians 5:21). On the cross the Lord Jesus Christ was the cursed one, vile, foul and repulsive in the sight of God. We all know what it is to feel guilty. It is an awful feeling to be wracked by guilt. So we cannot begin to imagine how Christ must have felt when he was taking the blame for the sins of millions and God reckoned these sins as belonging to Christ.

Atonement

As well as making God angry, my sins also put me in debt with God, a debt that I would spend eternity in Hell paying off. But on the cross when Jesus cried out *It is finished* (John 19:30) he made full atonement for these sins.

Atonement means 'a making at one' and points to a process of bringing those who are estranged into unity. In theology (the study of God), it denotes the work of Christ in dealing with the problem of our sin and in bringing sinners into a right relationship with God.

The atonement he made was in the place of others. On the cross he was putting right, making up, paying a debt on behalf of all those who trust him. All our sins were laid on Christ (Isaiah 53:6, 12; John 1:29; 2 Corinthians 5:21; Galatians 3:13; Hebrews 9:28; 1 Peter 2:24). He took upon himself all my sins and paid for them all, every last one of them. The secret ones, the 'little' ones, the shameful ones, the ones I commit time and time and time again. The ones I have forgotten. The wilful ones. Finished! There is no more debt to pay.

There was once a chief of a tribe who was just and good. Someone in the tribe had been stealing and the chief said that whoever it was must be beaten. The thief turned out to be his elderly, frail mother. But justice had to be done. They tied her to the pole and were just about to beat her when the chief cried out, 'stop!' He got up and walked towards the pole and took off his shirt. He wrapped himself around her and said, 'Proceed.' On Calvary justice had to be done. A price had to be paid. A debt had to be settled. Someone had to take a beating. But for every man and woman, boy and girl who trusts in Jesus Christ, he wrapped himself around you on Calvary and said to God, 'Proceed.' The beating is over. The debt we owe has been fully paid. The wrath has been expended. It is finished!

Justification

When Jesus cried out 'It is finished' it meant that everything that needed to be done to put us right with God had been done. The Bible calls this 'justification.' Justification frees a person from the guilt of sin and its condemnation. It is a judicial act of God where he pardons sinners. He declares the sinner righteous;, perfect in his sight.

For me to be right with God I must keep God's law perfectly, in thought, word and deed. But it is impossible. I break it every day and there is nothing I can do to atone for all the sins I have committed.

All I can offer God is a bad record. Far from putting me right with God, the law and my attempts at keeping it confirm I am guilty and deserve God's wrath. It is impossible for me to be justified before God by the law. But based on what Christ did on Calvary, God is able to justify me.

Justification makes no actual change in me. It is a declaration by God concerning me. It is not something I get from what I do but rather something that is done for me. I have only been made righteous in the sense that God regards me as righteous and pronounces me righteous. As soon as I am justified I am right with God.

On the cross Jesus Christ was my substitute and took my place. In a legal sense, in God's eyes, he became me and I became him. Jesus lived a perfect life. This is called his active obedience. By trusting in him the life he lived becomes mine, his righteousness becomes mine. I take off the sinful life I have lived and put it on Jesus and he clothes me with his righteousness. When you stand before God, whose lifelong record would you rather rely on, yours or Jesus Christ's?

If you are a Christian you do not need to worry about standing before God on judgement day. You will stand before him clothed in the righteousness of Christ, as if you had done nothing wrong. We are accepted by God in Christ (Ephesians 1:6).

When I stand before God there will be many people who know me who could present a case as to why I should not be allowed into Heaven. People I grew up with, went to school with, went to university with, worked with, my family, friends who could all point to my sins and say, 'there's no way he should be allowed into Heaven.' There is my conscience that can bring to mind the things I have thought and done that no one else knows. That will definitely condemn me! On top of all that, God's law shows me I've failed on every point. The devil through all of these things will accuse me. But on that awesome day when I stand before the judge of all the earth, Jesus Christ will plead for me. He will stand with me and when the devil, the law, my conscience, my past and everyone who knows me will condemn me, he will say as it were: 'Look at the cross. On that I took all your sins upon myself and paid for every one of them!'

I taught a boy whose father was a bit of a small time crook. He and his mate once broke into a factory in Cwmbran in South Wales and stole a load of materials. They were caught red-handed but they managed to get a hot-shot lawyer to represent them. They went to court and stood in the dock and the lawyer made the case for their defence. He said that there was no way his clients could have been in the factory on that particular night and no way could they have taken the materials they were accused of taking. His case was so powerful and convincing that the boy's father turned to his mate and said, 'perhaps we didn't do it!'

On judgement day, when everyone will stand before God's judgement seat, Christians will have someone far greater pleading their eternal cause for them. They will turn to each other and say, 'it's like we didn't do it.'

Forgiveness

Christ was on the cross for six hours. During that time, he made seven utterances. The first was a prayer to God the Father, *Father, forgive them for they do not know what they do* (Luke 23:34). The Greek can be translated, 'Jesus kept on praying, "forgive them, forgive them, forgive them."' The Lord Jesus was on the cross to bring forgiveness to people who didn't deserve it, hell-deservers like you and I. There he paid for all the offences of his people against God so that all sin can be forgiven. Gossip, dirty thoughts, adultery, hatred, lying, lust, spitefulness, anger, laziness—all the mess, the tangled up lives and iniquities were laid on him (Isaiah 53:5).

> All my sin of every kind
> All the thoughts that stain
>   the mind
> All the evil I designed
> Laid on him
> All that sinks me in the mire
> All the times of base desire
> All that needs a cleansing fire
> Laid on him

LANCE PIBWORTH

Cleansing

As well as forgiveness, what Jesus did on the cross means that we can be made clean. 1 John 1:7 says, *the blood of Jesus Christ His Son cleanses us from all sin.* Our dirty hearts and filthy lives can be made clean. The late Rev Vernon Higham, former minister of the Heath Evangelical Church in Cardiff, on more than one occasion referred to a prostitute who attended church in the 1980s. She had lived a particularly dirty life but had started attending the Heath Church and realised her sinfulness and trusted the Lord Jesus Christ to save her. She would go back where she was staying with many other women who would taunt her that someone like her should never be going to church and that she could never be forgiven with her past. She felt hopeless and unclean. But she told Mr Higham that one night and a particularly bad evening, it was like the Lord Jesus Christ himself drew near to her and said 'in my sight you are a chaste virgin.'

And the cure works!

You may be reading this and thinking to yourself, 'but how do I know that what Jesus Christ did on the cross can cure the problem of my heart. How do I know his death on the cross can put me in a right relationship with God, bring me forgiveness and cleansing and pay the debt of all my sin and shame? How do I know this cure works?' Because amazingly and supernaturally, three days after Jesus died, he rose again! Jesus' resurrection declares sin has been dealt with, punishment is over. The Christian message is really 'about a divine Galilean whose heart pumped blood again, whole lungs filled with oxygen again, and whose synapses started firing again' (DeYoung, *Good News We Almost Forgot*, p91).

Theories that just don't stack up

However, many people try to convince us that this didn't happen, and come up with alternative theories of what actually took place.

Some argue he wasn't really dead when he was taken down from the cross and he simply revived in a cold tomb. But this really doesn't stand up. Jesus was crucified with two criminals and the Jews didn't want dead bodies remaining on the crosses on their holy day, the Sabbath. They asked Pilate that their legs might be broken and that they might be taken away. So the soldiers came and broke the legs of the first criminal and of the other but when they came to Jesus and saw that he was already dead they did not break his legs. But one of the soldiers pierced his side with a spear and at once there came out blood and water (John 19:31-34). Mark tells us, *Pilate marvelled that He was already dead; and summoning the centurion, he asked him if He had been dead for some time. So when he found out from the centurion, he granted the body to Joseph* (Mark 15:44-45). Pilate, the centurion and the soldiers all confirm he was dead!

Others argue that the women who found the empty tomb went to the wrong tomb. But surely this is clutching at straws, as the women saw where Joseph of Arimathea laid him (Luke 23:55). They watched closely as Jesus was laid in the tomb.

Another theory put forward is that the disciples came and stole his body. But this was impossible as there was no way out of the tomb: the Jewish leaders had gone to great lengths to secure it. They asked Pilate to order the tomb to be secure until the third day in case his disciples go and steal him away and tell the people *He has risen from the dead*. So Pilate ordered the guard to make the tomb as secure as they could. It was sealed by twine or cord, covered with pitch or clay and attached it to the front of the tomb so they would know in a minute if someone had tampered with it.

Then they took a guard of soldiers (between twelve and sixty men) to keep watch on the site. The soldiers would have thought it was the easiest task they had ever been assigned. Go to a garden and guard a tomb! They would not be expecting anything to happen. Just sit in a quiet garden for a day or two. But it proved to be an impossible task.

They might just as well have been told to go outside and stop the sun from rising!

After Jesus rose from the dead some of the guards hurried over to the chief priests to report what had happened (Matthew 28:11, 12). They didn't all go. They had been scattered in all directions and some would have been too scared to face the authorities. The chief priests quickly assembled with the elders to decide what to do next. They bribed the soldiers to spread the rumour that Jesus' disciples had come and stolen the body while they slept, and they promised that if news of them sleeping while the body was stolen reached Pilate, they would intercede for them (Matthew 28:14).

But all of this shows the utter foolishness of unbelief. The theory of the disciples coming and stealing the body is impossible but many would rather believe that between twelve and sixty well-trained Roman soldiers slept while eleven Galilean fishermen got past them, moved a big stone, unwrapped the body of Jesus, folded up the grave clothes and then walked out of the tomb carrying the body. They must have been the best sleepers ever! And where their story really falls down is that if anyone asked them what happened their answer was that while they were sleeping, his disciples came and stole the body. That begs the immediate question, "if you were sleeping, how do you know what happened?"

Compelling Evidence

As well as the weakness of alternative theories, there is also other compelling evidence to prove the resurrection true.

Firstly, the women who went to the tomb and saw him alive. If his disciples had made it all up they would never have chosen women to be the first to have seen him. In first century Israel it was impossible for women to give testimony in court because their word could not legally be trusted. If someone was going to make something up the first rule would be, 'Don't use women as witnesses.'

Furthermore, if they had made it up surely they would have embellished the story. They would have described the resurrection itself, the descent of the angel, moving the stone, the appearance of the Lord Jesus from within the recess of the tomb. The apocryphal gospels (false stories that circulated that were given impressive names, such as the Gospel according to Hebrews, the Gospel of Peter, Acts of Pilate and others) contain elements of how Jesus appeared to Pilate and confounded him, or how he appeared to Caiaphas and other members of the Jewish Sanhedrin. The Gospel writers in the Bible don't include any of these 'juicy' bits. Why? Because they had no interest in adding to the truth. The Gospels do not describe the resurrection because no one actually witnessed it, even though it would have made good copy. They just say what they saw.

Another compelling argument is the effect it

had on the disciples. How did they go from being paralysed with fear, hiding behind locked doors, too scared to come out, to boldly preaching on the streets of Jerusalem? The disciples who ran at the first sign of trouble would not have died for what they knew was a fabrication. It was not in their minds that he could rise from the dead. Even after the women told the eleven disciples and the rest of the followers of Jesus in the locality, the males still thought the story *idle tales* and didn't believe them (Luke 24:10-11). Peter saw the empty tomb, but could not take it all in (Luke 24:12). As the news begun to spread, by and large it was not accepted as true. As the commentator Leon Morris says:

> The apostles were not men poised on the brink of belief and needing only the shadow of an excuse before launching forth into a proclamation of resurrection. They were utterly sceptical. Clearly, irrefutable evidence was needed to convince these sceptics.

But the most compelling argument, one that could settled everything in the first century, is the body. If the authorities could have produced the body of Jesus they would undoubtedly have done so, for it would have settled everything in their favour. A Hindu and a Christian were travelling together on a boat. As they sailed past a certain place the Hindu turned to the Christian and said, "Over there are buried the bones of my saviour." The Christian replied, "If you could find the bones of my Saviour, he wouldn't be my Saviour!"

The fact is, Jesus Christ is alive and what he accomplished on the cross can cure the problem of your heart. Christians are not people who are following someone who lived 2000 years ago. Our Saviour is a living Saviour. No thinking person really asks if it is true anymore. No one buys the theories that he fainted and was resuscitated or the disciples stole him. Christianity stands up to rigorous investigation. The real reason people don't believe it is because they do not want to believe. There are always people like that, but like people who smoke and ignore the health evidence, they are closing their eyes to truth and heading for ruin. It's the easy way out. But you must not allow yourself just to take the easy way out: your eternal destiny hangs on it.

THE DOCTOR

The symptoms are obvious, the diagnosis rings true. The prognosis is frightening, but the cure is amazing. All you need to do is come to the doctor and let him do his work. But I imagine some of you still feel you can't, or won't, for all kinds of reasons.

Too frightened to go to the doctor

Some of you worry about coming to Jesus Christ and believe that he won't help you. Perhaps you feel you are too bad to be cured. But this doctor is tender and caring and kind. The Bible says he is rich in mercy and abounding in grace, and grace means undeserved kindness.

In Mark 7:31-37 there is an account of when Jesus healed a deaf man. He took him aside from the crowd privately. He is going to make this man hear for the first time—the man had never heard a noise and Jesus doesn't want it to be too noisy for him the first time he can hear, so he takes him away from the crowd. He doesn't want him to be alarmed so he uses sign language to explain what he is about to do by putting his fingers in his ears and after spitting touched his tongue.

Another example is in Mark 9:14-29. Jesus heals a boy with an unclean spirit. Jesus asked the father, 'How long has this been happening to him?' He is interested. He says to this heartbroken, beside-himself father, 'tell me your story; tell me all about it.' If you come to Jesus Christ he will deal with you patiently and tenderly. You don't need to be afraid.

A man would have his hair cut in a certain barber's shop in Australia. The man was a Christian but the barber who always cut his hair was very dismissive about the things of God and would make fun of him. One day he went to have his haircut but the barber was not there. He asked the other gentleman cutting his hair where he was and was told that he had finished work because he had found out he had terminal cancer and didn't have much time left. As the man walked out of the shop he saw his old barber sat in his car crying his eyes out. The man went over to him and the old barber said, 'For 40 years I kicked him in the face but the minute I called to him he came to me.' The God of the Bible is a big hearted, compassionate God who will abundantly pardon (Isaiah 55:7).

Too bad to be cured

Some of you are convinced that your hearts are too bad to be cured. There is a verse in the Bible that really troubles people. It is in Matthew 12:31-32 and says:

> Therefore I say to you, every sin and blasphemy will be forgiven men, but the blasphemy against the Spirit will not be forgiven men. Anyone who speaks a word against the Son of Man, it will be forgiven him; but whoever speaks against the Holy Spirit, it will not be forgiven him, either in this age or in the age to come

But if we look at the verse closely, it is actually a really encouraging verse. It says, *every sin and blasphemy will be forgiven men.* **Everything** you have done can be forgiven, with only one exception. That one thing is to refuse the work of the Holy Spirit, who draws us to repent and believe on the Lord Jesus Christ. To refuse the work of the Holy Spirit, and that alone, is unforgivable.

On the side of a plumber's van in Coventry it said, 'No hole too dark, too dirty or too deep that we can't reach.' There is no heart too dark, too dirty or too deep that God's love can't reach.

You are a rotten sinner. Like me, I am sure many of you have committed awful sins, wilful sins, shameful sins. But God is gracious; he shows us undeserved kindness. The Bible says that where sin abounds, grace abounds all the more. God is more gracious than you are sinful. I remember when my son was very little and I was by the sea with him. He started to run down the jetty towards the sea. As he ran he got faster and faster and faster and couldn't stop. But I ran down the jetty after him and being quicker caught up with him and stopped him. Your sin is fast. It abounds quickly, it may have already run away with you. But God's grace abounds even faster and can outrun your sin.

However bad a sinner you are, he is a better saviour than you are a sinner. He is more gracious than you are sinful.

Waiting until you get better before you go to the doctor

Some of you may think that you have to get yourself better before you come. Some of you may be in a relationship or family situation where you've messed up. Some in emotional trauma; some in grief and sorrow or the clutches of temptation. Some of you have ruined your reputations. Some of you may have committed a 'big' sin that haunts you. You are in a mess. Maybe you imagine a pure and holy God must be completely uninterested in someone like you. You are quite wrong: you must come to him, just as you are. He is far more willing to receive you than you are to come to him.

My dad was a minister in Pontypridd. A tramp called Frank would come in every Sunday night to listen to him preach. He was an alcoholic, reeked of drink, dirty and scruffy. After a while, Frank suddenly stopped coming. A few months later dad was in his car and saw him standing waiting for the bus in the pouring rain. My dad pulled over and told him to get in. He said "Where have you been, Frank? We've missed you." Frank said that a couple of the deacons had told him to stop coming to church until he cleaned himself up and stopped smelling of drink! Those deacons were completely wrong, and so are you if you think like they did. I tell you on the authority of God's Word, come to Jesus Christ as you are; in a mess, smelling of drink, covered in sin, it doesn't matter. Simply ask him to save you.

The Lord Jesus Christ says, *The one who comes to me I will by no means cast out'* (John 6:37). You can trust his word. It is not my invitation, it is his. You can be sure of his word and trust your eternal soul on it! The famous writer of *The Pilgrim's Progress*, John Bunyan, started off by praying, 'forgive me my sins, I'll try harder tomorrow' but ended up praying, 'I can't be any better please save me.' And God did, so why not you?

Ignore the need to go to the doctor

Others of you will just ignore the problem. You don't want to think about it and try to convince yourself it is not true. But one day you will have to die and face up to it. As George Bernard Shaw put it, *Life's ultimate statistic is the same for all people: one out of one dies.* Our sense of permanence is an illusion.

You cannot afford to take any chances with your never-dying soul. A story is told of a man who sold everything he had to buy a precious diamond. He was on a the deck of a ship one day tossing the diamond up in the air and catching it, tossing it up in the air and catching it. A lady approached him and told him how foolish he was being and how he needed to take care of something so precious. He laughed and told her to stop worrying and that he had been doing it for ages and it was fine. He threw the diamond up again but suddenly the boat jerked and the diamond fell into the water. The man screamed at the top of his voice, 'Lost! Lost! Everything is lost!' Maybe you are playing with your soul and you've been doing it for ages and it's fine. But God will suddenly say your soul is required of you and you'll spend eternity screaming 'Lost! Lost! Everything is lost!'

A particular reason you won't come to the doctor

But in all likelihood, the reason you won't come to the doctor is because there is a sin you love too much and you are not ready to choose between Jesus Christ and your sin. You think that you can have sin for a while and then sort out your eternal soul later. Maybe it is a sexual sin. Maybe it is popularity—you look at Christ and then look at your friends, family, colleagues, fellow students, teachers, society and think 'I don't want to become unpopular.' Maybe you don't want to lose power or possessions or privileges. But as the Lord Jesus Christ said, *For what profit is it to a man if he gains the whole world, and loses his own soul? Or what will a man give in exchange for his soul?* (Matthew 16.26). The bottom line is this: is whatever you are clinging to worth going to Hell for?

There will never be a more convenient time than now. Every day you carry on in your sin it takes more and more of a hold of you. Every day you carry on in your sin you harden your heart until there comes that point of no return when God hardens it and you are lost (Exodus 9:12).

Come to the doctor!

Just come to the doctor! The way you come to him is in repentance and faith. That is, you have to be sorry for your sin and willing to turn away from it and trust in what Jesus did on the cross. Whatever you have done, however tangled and messed up your life is, however full of pride and scornful and hateful towards God you have been, you can come to him now. Meet him at the cross: Jesus doesn't meet people in offices behind big desks; the only place he has appointed is at the cross.

You must tell him everything, look into your

heart, leave no place out of bounds to him. It will be painful but it is the only way to be fully restored and have intimate communion with the Saviour. Examine your heart (Lamentations 3:40). Confess and repent of any known sin (1 John 1:8-9). Whatever you have done, if you come to him in repentance and faith, he will save you.

Every religion in the world says that to be right with God you must do something. Keep certain food laws, wear certain clothes, follow certain rules, fast for one month of the year during sunlight, go on pilgrimages, bathe in a particular river, confess your sins to a priest, 'do, do, do.' And even then you can't be certain, but Christianity says with a loud voice, 'Done!' Everything's been done for you. Trust in a finished work.

A story is told of a young Irish boy who went along to a mission to hear a famous evangelist preach about Hell and sin and judgement and the need to be saved. The mission lasted a week and as the week went on the boy became more and more troubled. After the last meeting he went home and couldn't sleep. Over and over in his mind went the question 'what must I do to be saved? What must I do?' The following morning he got up straight away and ran back to the field where the mission had been held. The organisers were taking the tents down and packing up. After looking frantically, the young boy finally found the evangelist. He said to him, 'Sir, what must I do to be saved? What must I do?' The evangelist said to him, 'You're too late son.

You're too late! In fact you are two thousand years too late. It's all been done for you.' Trust in a finished work! Say with the Christian hymn writer,

> Upon a life I did not live,
> Upon a death I did not die;
> Another's life, another's death,
> I stake my whole eternity.

Maybe you've been trying to save yourself. You've tried turning over a new leaf, giving up some bad habits, going to church, reading your Bible, even trying to pray, but none of it seems to be working. You keep wondering if you've done enough and are always worried about that one dreadful thing you did in your past. Let me tell you what the great Martin Luther was told:

> Look at the wounds of Jesus Christ, to the blood He has shed for you. Instead of torturing yourself on account of your sins, throw yourself into the Redeemer's arms.

Faith really means to take God at his word. It is believing what he promised and trusting in what he has done. You have to know certain things and believe them to be true: you are a sinner and need to be saved, you cannot save yourself and that Jesus Christ is the Son of God and the only Saviour. You then have to trust your whole life to him. Throw your whole self upon him. Your past, your present and your future. You stop trusting yourself and trust him.

And real faith is inextricably linked to repentance. If I have real faith in Jesus Christ and totally trust in him then I will repent. That means I will turn away from my sin and my old way of life. As Jim Packer has written:

> The New Testament word for repentance means changing one's mind so that one's views, values, goals and ways are changed and one's whole life is lived differently. The change is radical, both inwardly and outwardly; mind and judgement, will and affections, behaviour and life style, motives and purposes, are all involved. Repentance means starting to live a new life.

Just come. Face up to who you really are, not who you want to be, who you are trying to be or want others to think that you are, but who you are. Tony Adams, the ex-England and Arsenal captain, visited the Fulham Boys School a few years ago. While we chatted in my office he told me how his life had once been ruined by alcohol. He hit rock bottom. He attended an alcoholics anonymous meeting where he sat in a circle and said, "My name is Tony Adams and I am an alcoholic." He was

England captain, had won the double with Arsenal, was an Arsenal legend, but when you stripped it all away, his name was Tony and he was an alcoholic! I can try and define and describe myself in lots of ways, but the truth is my name is Alun Ebenezer and I am a sinner. Don't pretend to be something that you are not. Own up to what you are.

The heart of the problem is the problem of the heart. The symptoms are obvious. The diagnosis spot on. The prognosis is terrifying. The cure sublime. And the doctor is ready and willing to see you... Come to him now!

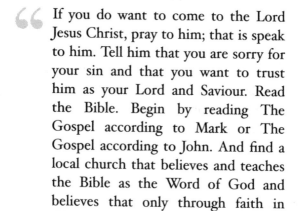

If you do want to come to the Lord Jesus Christ, pray to him; that is speak to him. Tell him that you are sorry for your sin and that you want to trust him as your Lord and Saviour. Read the Bible. Begin by reading The Gospel according to Mark or The Gospel according to John. And find a local church that believes and teaches the Bible as the Word of God and believes that only through faith in Christ alone can a person be right with God.

ACKNOWLEDGEMENTS

Books

Bunyan, J. (1997) Pilgrims Progress. Banner of Truth Trust. Edinburgh.

DeYoung, K. (2010) The Good News We Almost Forgot. Moody Publishers. Chicago

Leahy, F.S. (1999) Great Conversions. Ambassador. Belfast.

Morris, L. (2008) Tynedale New Testament Commentaries Luke. IVP

Packer, J.I. (1993) Concise Theology. IVP. Leicester, England

Articles

Minnesota Crime Commission Report (1926) Printed in the Journal of the American Institute of Criminal Law and Criminology 18, no1 (May 1927)

Newspapers/Magazines

The Times (July 29th 2008)

The Times (November 21st 2009)
The Week (12th September 2015)